Secrets To Organizing The Perfect Speech

How to organize the best speech of your life!

"*Practical, proven techniques that will help you to organize your next speech to make it a success*"

Dr. Jim Anderson

Published by:

Blue Elephant Consulting
Tampa, Florida

Copyright © 2013 by Dr. Jim Anderson

All rights reserved. No part of this book may be reproduced of transmitted in any form or by any means, electronic or mechanical, including photocopying, recording or by any information storage and retrieval system without written permission of the publisher, except for inclusion of brief quotations in a review.

Printed in the United States of America

Library of Congress Control Number: 2013919455

ISBN-13: 978-1493588817

ISBN-10: 1493588818

Warning – Disclaimer

The purpose of this book is to educate and entertain. This book does not promise or guarantee that anyone following the ideas, tips, suggestions, techniques or strategies will be hired. It is the discretion of employers if you will or will not be hired. The author, publisher and distributor(s) shall have neither liability nor responsibility to anyone with respect to any loss or damage caused, or alleged to be caused, directly or indirectly by the information contained in this book.

Other Books By The Author

- How To Have A Successful Product Manager Career: The Things That You Need To Be Doing TODAY In Order To Have A Successful Product Manager Career

- Product Manager Product Success: How to keep your product on track and make it become a success

- Secrets To Planning The Perfect Speech

- IT Manager Budgeting Skills

- CIO Business Skills: How CIOs can work effectively with the rest of the company!

- Preparing For Your Next Negotiation: What You Need To Do BEFORE A Negotiation Starts In Order To Get The Best Possible Deal

- Power Distribution Unit (PDU) Secrets: What Everyone Who Works In A Data Center Needs To Know!

- Making The Jump: How To Land Your Dream Job When You Get Out Of College!

Acknowledgements

Any book like this one is the result of years of real-world work experience. In my over 25 years of working for 7 different firms, I have met countless fantastic people and I've been mentored by some truly exceptional ones. Although I've probably forgotten some of the people who made me the person that I am today, here is my attempt to finally give them the recognition that they so truly deserve:

- Thomas P. Anderson
- Art Puett
- Bobbi Marshall
- Bob Boggs

Dr. Jim Anderson

This book is dedicated to my wife Lori. None of this would have been possible without her love and support.

Thanks for the best 21 years of my life (so far)...!

Table Of Contents

WHAT'S THE BEST WAY ORGANIZE A GREAT SPEECH? 7

ABOUT THE AUTHOR 8

HOW TO GET YOUR MESSAGE TO STICK WITH EVERYONE! 12

I SAY HELLO, YOU SAY GOODBYE… 16

HUH? LEARNING TO STAY IN THE MOMENT 19

GROUP MEETINGS: GROUP HUG OR GROUP MUG(GING)? 22

GROUP MEETINGS: MORE GAIN, LESS PAIN 26

HOW SHOULD I INTRODUCE YOU PUBLIC SPEAKER? 29

BACK TO BASICS: PRESENTATION TIPS 101 33

A PRESENTER'S POWERPOINT SLIDES: TOO LITTLE OF A BAD THING? 37

MAKE YOUR AUDIENCE SIT UP, TAKE NOTICE, AND LEARN AT YOUR NEXT PRESENTATION 40

7 SECRETS TO GETTING YOUR ADULT AUDIENCE TO LEARN FROM YOUR PRESENTATION 43

THE PRESENTER'S DILEMMA: 5 WAYS TO MAKE YOUR TRAINING STICK 46

JUST HOW DO THOSE POLITICIANS DO IT? 49

What's The Best Way Organize A Great Speech?

So you've been asked to give a speech – fantastic! Just think of all of the great speakers who have gone before you Dr. Martin Luther King, John F. Kennedy, Steve Jobs, the list goes on and on. Now you've been give your chance to change the world!

I can well image what you are feeling right now – fear, doubt, uncertainty. Don't worry about it. I've got good news for you – all of those great speakers felt the very same thing. However, they were able to muster up the courage to go out there and give the best speech that they possibly could. They did change the world and you just might end up doing the same thing.

However, before you go doing that, we've got to make sure that you've got a well-planned speech to work with. Organizing a speech is the first step in creating and delivering a powerful and effective speech. In order to organize a speech you need to take the time before you start to clearly identify why you are the person that your audience should be listening to and then create an outline of the speech that you want to give.

When organizing a speech you need to make sure that you have a strong opening. The body of your speech has to build toward your closing. Finally, the closing has to leave your audience with something that they'll be able to remember long after your speech is over and done with.

The good news is that I know that you're going to give a great speech and it's all going to start with the organizing. Read this book, learn what you need to do in order to organize a great speech and then go out there and knock 'em dead!

Good luck!

- Dr. Jim Anderson, October, 2013

About The Author

I must confess that I never set out to be a public speaker. When I went to school, I studied Computer Science and thought that I'd get a nice job programming and that would be that. Well, at least part of that plan worked out!

My first job was working for Boeing on their F/A-18 fighter jet program. I spent my days programming fighter jet software in assembly language and I loved it. The U.S. government decided to save some money and went looking for other countries to sell this plane to. This put me into an unfamiliar role: I started to meet with foreign military officials and I ended up having to give speeches in order to explain what my product did.

Time moved on and so did I. I found myself working for Siemens, the big German telecommunications company. They were making phone switches and selling them to the seven U.S. phone companies. The problem was that the switches were too complicated. Customers couldn't tell the difference between one complicated phone switch from another complicated phone switch. Once again I found myself standing in front of the room giving speeches in order to explain what these complicated machines did and why ours were better than anyone else's.

I've spent over 25 years working as a product manager for both big companies and startups. This has given me an opportunity to do many, many presentations for customers, at conferences, and everywhere in-between.

I now live in Tampa Florida where I spend my time managing my consulting business, Blue Elephant Consulting, teaching college courses at the University of South Florida, and traveling to work with companies like yours to share the knowledge that I have about how to create and deliver powerful and effective speeches.

I'm always available to answer questions and I can be reached at:

Dr. Jim Anderson
Blue Elephant Consulting
Email: jim@BlueElephantConsulting.com
Facebook: http://goo.gl/1TVoK
Web: http://www.BlueElephantConsulting.com/

"Unforgettable communication skills that will set your ideas free…"

Create Speeches That Motivate Your Audiences And Get Your Message Heard!

Dr. Jim Anderson is available to provide training and coaching on the topics that are the most important to people who have to speak in public: how can I create a speech that people want to hear and how can I deliver in a way that will allow me to connect with my audience and get my point across to them?

Dr. Anderson believes that in order to both learn and remember what he says, speakers need to laugh. Each one of his speeches is full of fun and humor so that what he says "sticks" with everyone.

Dr. Anderson's Public Speaking Training Includes:

1. How to plan your next speech: pick your purpose and understand your audience.
2. What's the best way to get PowerPoint and Keynote to work with you, not against you?
3. What do you need to do when you are presenting in order to truly connect with your audience?

Dr. Jim Anderson presents over 100 speeches per year. To invite Dr. Anderson to speak at your event, contact him at:

Phone: 813-418-6970 or
Email: jim@BlueElephantConsulting.com

Blue Elephant Consulting

Speaking.   Negotiating.   Managing.   Marketing.

Chapter 1

How To Get Your Message To Stick With Everyone!

How To Get Your Message To Stick With Everyone!

How many times has this happened: you've got an important message to get across, you work hard to put together the best presentation that you can, you practice-practice-practice, and then when you finally deliver your pièce de résistance you can clearly see that some folks in the audience are getting it while others have tuned you out. Dang it! What can you do to reach everyone?

You've already learned how to connect with your audience. Now it's time to find a way to get your message to stick. The good news here is that it's not your fault. What's going on is that you are trying to communicate with a group of adults and they all have different learning styles.

We all have our own personal style by which we learn and too often we assume that that is how the rest of the world learns also. Hmm, sure sounds like we've got to figure out how adults learn.

My buddy Lenn Millbower is an expert in this area and he refined his tactics while working for Disney so you know he's got to be good. At the root of what Lenn teaches is that us adults fall into four basic groups of learning styles (see if you can pick yours out):

1. **Act / Think: "Lab Style"** – this is where much of an technical audience ends up. These folks like to test the new information by solving problems, being objective, seeking results, experimenting, and tinkering.

2. **Act / Feel: "Playground Style"** – this type of learner really likes to try out the new information that is being taught. Doing things like acting, sensing, deciding, applying, and then connecting ideas all help to make what's being taught "stick".

3. **Reflect / Feel: "Cafe Style"** – you'll find this type of crowd down at your local Starbucks if you don't do something to hold their attention. They like to talk about your information once you have shared it. This includes sharing, relating, discussing, seeking attention, and working in groups.

4. **Reflect / Think: "Lecture Hall Style"** – yep, this is the "old school" style that we all grew up with. For some, it works the best. It is based on thinking about what is being taught. Your audience then likes to listen to experts, explore principles, analyze ideas, theorize, and of course read.

These four groups are at the heart of the 4MAT approach to teaching. I can hear you now: so I've got an audience made up of four different learning styles, how am I supposed to reach out to all of them? It sounds like I really need four different presentations. No you don't. Instead, what you need to do is to make sure that you present your main points in four different ways within the same single presentation.

That's right, rotate through each of the four learning styles so that you make sure that you get through to your audience. Real quickly, let's look at an example.

Let's say that your company has just bought another company and you are in charge of merging the two sets of billing applications that the two companies currently use. If you were giving a kick-off presentation to both company's IT departments, then you'd want to do the following: clearly define the problem that integrating the multiple billing systems presents and ask the audience to think about how they'd tackle this problem (Lab Style), show how combining billing systems will streamline the new company's ordering process (Playground Style), divide the audience up into groups in order to create a list of the top 10 issues that will need to be tackled (Cafe Style), and have someone who has done this type of IT project before say some words about what to watch out for (Lecture Hall Style).

If you can work these four different approaches to presenting the same material into a single presentation, then you'll have solved the problem of getting your message to "stick" with everyone in your audience.

Chapter 2

I Say Hello, You Say Goodbye...

I Say Hello, You Say Goodbye…

Whenever we are called on to give a speech or write a report, we almost always focus on what we'd like to say in the middle of the delivery of our material. What's interesting is that no matter if we are speaking the words or writing them, it's the way that we start and the way that we wrap things up that really makes the most lasting impression.

That being said, just how do you go about creating an introduction to your material that will (1) capture their attention and (2) make them eager for more? Oh yeah, how do you go about wrapping things up in such a way that you let your audience / reader know that the conclusion is coming?

When talking about opening, middle, and conclusion of your material it is almost impossible to avoid references to food. Whether it's sandwiches (two pieces of bread and a filling) or a salad / main course / desert, the analogies can run wild.

No matter which one you pick, the references are a valid way of reminding you that your opening and closing will be what holds your material together. Here are five tried and true "recipes" for creating openings and closings that will help your audience / readers to remember what you are telling them:

1. **Challenging Opening Statement**: If you use a thought-provoking or intriguing statement to start your material off, you can "hook" your reader's interest from the get-go. A statement like "Without new products, our company will be forced to close its doors in two years" is guaranteed to catch someone's attention. If used, then you must reference this statement in your conclusion so that the circle is closed for your reader: "So while the company requires a steady stream of new products, this product is well suited to be included in that group."

2. **Startling Statistics**: Using a statistic that the audience / reader is not aware of is a great attention grabber. In

order to make this an even more powerful tool, cite one or more well-known statistics before you unveil the startling statistic. This will serve to increase the audience's surprise. Example: "Most IT staffers believe reports that say that most large IT projects fail. The truth is that only about 15% of IT projects completely fail." Once again, the statistic that is discussed in the opening must once again be discussed in your closing.

3. **Emotionally Appealing Short Story / Anecdote**: This can be especially powerful if your audience / readers believe that you are opening up to them. Talking about failures or successes that relate to your main topic is a great way to capture interest and build credibility. As always, remember to come back to this story when you are wrapping things up in your conclusion.

4. **Question**: Asking an open-ended question (key point) at the start of your material is a proven way to capture your audience / reader's attention. It forces them to think about what you are saying and decide how they would answer it. As always, make sure that you come back and provide an answer to this question in your conclusion.

5. **Compare or Contrast**: The human mind is designed to pick up on differences — it's probably what kept our ancestors alive longer. Starting your material with a comparison or a contrast between two things that your audience / reader is not aware of will make them want to learn more. Coming back to the comparison / contrast one more time the in the conclusion will help to drive home your main points.

This list of five ways to create a powerful opening / closing is by no means a complete list. However, you now have a good set of ways to frame your material in such a way that you've got better odds of making it stick. Please keep in mind that you can also blend these different approaches together to make an even more effective way to deliver your material.

Chapter 3

Huh? Learning To Stay In The Moment

Huh? Learning To Stay In The Moment

So there I was, on one of those conference calls with way too many people and all of a sudden it started to happen. The moderator would ask a question of someone who was on the call and that person would say "Huh? I'm sorry, but could you repeat the question?"

This happened over and over again with different people. I just sat there and thought to myself – "Man, is nobody paying attention to this call?" Although it sounds simple, it turns out that staying in the moment is getting more and more difficult to do…

What's really going on here? It's always been difficult to get people to remember & retain what has gone on it a meeting; however, now we seem to be having problems with people not being able to keep up with the flow of a meeting.

According to author Cherie Kerr we may have the wrong focus. Outside of those folks who are deliberately doing other work during a meeting (iPhone anyone?), the people who are actually trying to participate often make the mistake of focusing on the goals of the meeting instead of what is being said right now.

The real goal of a meeting is achieve some sort of result. This can be an agreement, determine a next step, or reach a decision. That's the end point. How you get there is the responsibility of the person who is running the meeting.

If that's you , then what you want to have happen is for everyone in the meeting to build on what has already been said instead of coming up with completely new directions for the meeting to head off in. Note that we're not talking about Brainstorming sessions here, but rather normal business meetings.

By building on top of what has already been said, there will be a clear path from where you started to where the goal of the meeting is. Each discussion in the meeting will have a clear start, middle, and end as you lead into the next conversation.

It will also quickly become clear if you've gone off the path and you'll be able to bring the meeting back in line. Your participants will be more engaged because they'll have a better understanding of where the meeting has been and where it is going.

This suggestion is not new. In fact the folks who do improv comedy do this all the time. Their skits flow from one character's actions to another's quickly. Hey, if it works for a 30 minute TV show, then surely it will work for your next business meeting!

Chapter 4

Group Meetings: Group Hug or Group Mug(ging)?

Group Meetings: Group Hug or Group Mug(ging)?

Every technical organization seems to have a big annual meeting of some sort. The last one of these that I attended was put on by an Executive Director at a firm who liked to do these twice a year. He would fly in all of his direct reports and have them spend 30 minutes each talking about what their team had accomplished.

Some awards were given out, the Executive Director spoke some words of encouragement and then his vice president who had also flown in for the meeting wrapped things up with a motivational talk. This took the better part of a full day and for the life of me, an hour after the meeting was over I could have told you how many emails I had waiting for me once I got back to the office, but not what was discussed.

The motivation for these meetings can be quite different from group to group or even from year to year; however, each meeting seems to be painfully familiar. Although the scope of the meeting often depends on the size of the company. Now that we've got the inner game of public speaking taken care of, let's talk about the outer game of how to throw a BIG meeting – those are often the biggest communications disasters.

What's the purpose of these meetings? Often the firm has so many different products / projects / programs that they decide that a big meeting is just the way to ensure that everyone knows what's going on at the company. These meetings are, on the surface, quite expensive to put on, and if you take an even closer look they turn out to be really, really expensive once you take into consideration the lost productivity that they cause. They could be a good use of time; however, here are a few reasons why they generally miss the mark:

1. **<u>Who You Talking To?</u>** Most of these organization meetings are planned and put on by the same set of folks (the people who drew the short straws). What this

means is that the topics that are covered and the sequence in which they are covered tends to be the same from meeting to meeting – why mess with success? How can you possibly expect an audience to "stay in the moment" for these types of presentations? What makes a great meeting is when controversial topics are included. Yes, this can be dangerous but that's exactly why people will remember them.

2. **My Way Or The Highway**. Who is invited to do what and how they are permitted to do it can be a real sticking point at these meetings. If every speaker is required to have 25 slides and to talk for 30 minutes and participate in one big panel session at the end, then congratulations – everyone is going to look the same and be forgotten just as quickly. If instead, each presenter is encouraged to do what they need to do in order to get their message across, then at least you'll have some variety. Sure, there will still be some with 25 slides and 30 minute presentations; however, you'll also have others that just might have their message stick.

3. **You're So Popular To Me**. Just because someone who is presenting during one of these meetings is popular, doesn't mean that anyone is learning anything. I have seen plenty of presentations where a well-liked manager delivers a presentation to a packed house. However, afterwords I realized that he/she really hadn't said anything. What a waste of time! Making sure that everyone has a point to their presentation is a key preparation step.

4. **Complex Meetings Need Simple Solutions**. The more complicated the subject matter, the more simple it must be for the audience to attend and to understand what is being discussed. If the discussion requires detailed charts or process flows, then make sure that handouts are available and that the slides only show a subset of the information – no need to remind your audience that they aren't getting any younger by

making them squint at tiny fonts on a screen all the way up at the front of the room. Likewise, if everyone is going to be in one room listening to one speaker who is talking about a complex subject, make sure that everyone can see the speaker – ensure that there is a raised platform. This will go a long way to help keep their interest.

5. **Watch Those Awards**. The one part of a meeting like this that can kill the whole deal is the awards show. This introduces two problems: first, they are boring and second, if I'm not winning an award then I'll start to resent the person who is. Keep in mind what you are trying to achieve with the whole meeting and make sure that an awards show fits. If it does, then make it like a hotel room tryst – quick, pleasant, and forgotten once it's done.

Chapter 5

Group Meetings: More Gain, Less Pain

Group Meetings: More Gain, Less Pain

We've talked about the fact that group meetings, especially for teams, can be a large expense and a big waste of time if not set up and run correctly. These are great opportunities to communicate with the entire team and you really don't want to blow it. If you get picked to set one of these meetings up, I've got just a few more suggestions on how to make the meeting memorable not a memorial.

1. **Bridge Virtual and Real Worlds**: All adults learn differently and they don't stop doing this just because there's a large group meeting going on. Blogs, podcasts, wikis all play a role in day-to-day life and have become the way that some team members prefer to learn.

    Don't fight this, instead embrace it. If you don't have time for everyone associated with a project to present their part of it, why not record a podcast and make it available to attendees to download. This way you can reduce the amount of time spent on that topic and yet still provide complete coverage. Use the tools to enhance the meeting experience.

2. **So What Did You Think About That?** Providing the audience with an opportunity to comment on speakers and sessions is the key to completing the circle. Especially with Gen-X & Gen-Y'ers there is a need to be able to provide feedback in order to feel as though their participation really counted for something. This also helps shape the next meeting by telling the organizer what worked and what just flat out bombed.

3. **Context Gives Meaning To Content**: Identify what you want the attendees to get out of attending the meeting. Why are they coming and what do you want them to be able to do when they leave? With this knowledge you can plan the day's events to start everyone out in the same place and then gradually lead them to where you want to get them too. This sure beats just throwing

together a bunch of speakers to fill a day.

4. **Is This Going To Be Graded?** How the meeting is viewed after it is all over will be the summation of how each individual speaker was viewed. You really want to get the audience's opinion of each speaker; however, having one of those one-size-fits-all speaker evaluation forms never really seems to provide any useful feedback. Instead, create a set of different evaluation forms based on the presenter's content – technical, motivational, strategic, etc. This way you can truly learn who made a difference with your audience.

Chapter 6

How Should I Introduce You Public Speaker?

How Should I Introduce You Public Speaker?

You know, it's always the little things that set the real pros apart from the rest of us. When it comes to speaking in public, having a really good introduction for yourself can be the key to getting your speech off to a great start. I must confess that I had forgotten just how powerful an introduction could be. It took a chance opportunity to attend a private show put on by Billy Crystal to really remind me why introductions are important and, when done correctly, just how powerful they can be.

I was out in Las Vegas attending the big EMC trade show and as part of the show they had the comedian Billy Crystal come in and put on a private show. So there I was along with 1,000's of other trade show attendees sitting in a mini-arena waiting for Billy to take the stage. All of a sudden, the lights went down, and the jumbo-tron TV screens on the stage lit up.

What happened next was the mini-movie that had been created to introduce Billy at the start of the 2004 Academy Awards played. This was a real movie – it must have lasted for just a bit over 5 minutes or so. It was also quite funny – Billy kept finding himself stuck inside a bunch of famous movies as it appeared as though people were trying to talk him into hosting the Academy Awards. Once the movie was over, Billy came out, took the stage, and put on a great show.

It wasn't until days later (sorry, I really am this slow sometimes) that I suddenly realized WHY the movie had been played. Billy Crystal is a comedian. Comedians (the big ones at least) never just come out and take the stage – they always have an opening act. Why you ask? Simple, the opening act gets the crowd warmed up. It gets them used to laughing.

This means that when the main act (the comedian) comes out, he/she doesn't have to work as hard to get laughs – we're already primed for them. Even if the opening act bombs, the main comedian will appear great in comparison and we'll still laugh much easier. Billy didn't have an opening act for the private show that he was putting on so Billy's intro movie got every laughing before he came out. It worked like a charm.

What we can all learn from this is that WE need an opening act before we start a speech. Even if other speakers have gone before us, we need our own personal opening act.

Good news, you don't have to go out and hire a comedian. All you have to do is write your own introduction and make sure that someone reads it just before you start your speech. If you've got a great intro, then the audience will be primed to hear what you are going to say. They'll view you as an expert and they will hang on your every word.

What Should Be In My Introduction? Your introduction serves two distinct and separate purposes: to establish your authority and to inform your audience why you are there. I'd suggest that you start by establishing your authority to be speaking on this topic. This can be fairly boring stuff so boil it down to what will impress this audience the most: any study that you've done, work experience, years in this field, etc. Next you want to explain why you are here today giving this speech. Just saying "my manager asked me to report on this topic" is not good enough. Ideally you'll explain that you are uniquely suited to discuss the issue, or that you have a deep motivation to resolve the problem. This serves as a great springboard into your actual speech.

How Long Should My Introduction Be? The shorter the better. When written out your introduction should be no longer than 1/2 of a typewritten page. Remember: from the audience's point-of-view your introduction is just answering the question "who is this person" – once they've got the info that they need, they'll stop listening.

Who Should Read My Introduction? This is the most important part. You're introduction needs to be read to the audience (off of the paper that you handed to him/her) by someone that the audience respects and accepts as one of their own. This will act as a bridge to your speech and will give you instant acceptance by the audience.

As simple as these steps to creating a powerful introduction may seem, there are still a number of potholes that can still screw things up. The #1 issue that I see come up time after time is that the person reading the introduction doesn't take the time to read it before the event, tries to wing it, and ends up flubbing it. Proper coordination with your introducer can minimize the chances of this happening.

Chapter 7

Back To Basics: Presentation Tips 101

Back To Basics: Presentation Tips 101

So perhaps you've had the opportunity to do some public speaking in the past, shucks maybe this is how you are currently making your living. As with all things that we've done a few (or many) times, we have a tendency to start to become just a little bit, how shall I say this, complacent?

I guess the word "lazy" would be just a bit too harsh, but I'm sure that you get the point. If our last presentation went over fairly well, then why rock the boat? Well, here's the harsh reality – you can do better. If you stall now, then you'll at best be as good as you were last time and in fact you'll probably start slipping and that won't be good for anyone.

In order to stop all of this from happening, let's take just a moment and see what David Brooks who once upon a time won the Toastmasters World Championship of Public Speaking contest can suggest to help us get better. David has seven presentation tips for us to remember and learn from:

1. **PowerPoint Is Really Not Your Friend:** Way too many of us spend more time working on the PowerPoint slides that we're going to use instead of working on what we are going to say (business presenters please confess NOW!) No matter how beautiful your slides are, nobody is going to remember them once your presentation is done. Don't hide behind your slides, instead let your slides support what you are saying.

2. **It's A Speech, Not A Battle:** All too often we approach a presentation just as though we are preparing to go to war with the audience. This is crazy – they are there because they want to hear what you have to say, not to throw stones at you. The most painful thing in the world for an audience is to sit through is a bad speech. Therefore, they are actually on your side. They may or may not agree with what you are talking about, but they want you to do a good job no matter what.

3. **Why Are You Doing This?:** Look, why are you going to be willing to stand in front of a group of people and talk to them? What is that reason? It can always be put into one or more of four buckets: to entertain, to inspire, to persuade, or to inform. You need to know the answer to this question BEFORE you start to speak so that you can make sure that your words will accomplish what you want them to do.

4. **W.I.I.F.M.?:** How long should your presentation be? Not too long! Your audience will be asking themselves What's In It For Me (WIIFM) even before you open your mouth. The last thing that you want to do is to sound like a high school Spanish teacher who is going over the irregular verbs. Instead, you want to engage your audience in what you are saying and have them feel that you are having a conversation one-on-one with them directly that lasts just the right amount of time.

5. **It's ALWAYS Story Time:** Brooks makes a great point when he boils public speaking down to this very, very simple formula: make a point, tell a story, make a point, tell a story. When you are done talking, your audience probably won't be able to remember your points. However, there is a very good chance that they will be able to remember your stories long after you are done. Don't use other people's stories, instead pay attention to your world and "see" you own stories.

6. **Write But Don't Read!:** If you want to get really good at giving a speech here's the secret: write it out word-for-word. Don't you dare read it to your audience word-for-word! Instead, edit what you've written over and over again until the words shine from being polished so much. Then practice, practice, practice. Once you've practiced enough, you won't need to read your speech word-for-word, the words will simply tumble from your mouth with only the slightest shove provided by notes on cards.

7. **Don't Forget The "P" Word:** That would be, of course, practice. In order to get the little things that make a speech great like pauses and your own natural rhythm correct, you need to practice your speech over and over again. Make sure that you say the speech out loud just like you'll say it on that special day so that you can hear how you sound and make any needed changes.

Chapter 8

A Presenter's PowerPoint Slides: Too Little Of A Bad Thing?

A Presenter's PowerPoint Slides:
Too Little Of A Bad Thing?

Hopefully by now everyone at least knows that you can seriously damage your audience if you create and use poorly designed PowerPoint(or Keynote!) slides. The number one offence that everyone seems to be able to agree on is that a slide that has been overloaded with text and numbers (a) doesn't work, and (b) puts your audience to sleep. Good news – this problem has been solved!

Olivia Mitchell who is a speaking coach out of New Zealand (was there ever a "Zealand"?) discovered a blog posting by Laura Bergells in which she laments the current state of PowerPoint presentations.

Laura's main point is that most people have gotten the message that too much information is a bad thing. However, she objects to the way that we are currently solving it – by removing basically all of the information from our PowerPoint slides and replacing it with pretty pictures.

She's got a good point – I've started doing this over the past year or so. However, in my own defense, I only started doing it because I saw that Steve Jobs had been doing it and everyone was just raving about his presentations.

I sorta don't have the heart to tell Laura that it's probably going to get worse (in her opinion) before it gets better. A new presentation format in which you only get twenty slides and can show each one for "only" twenty seconds (for a total of 6 minutes 40 seconds) is catching on. This presentation style is called Pecha Kucha, and was started by two architects in Tokyo as part of a designers' show-and-tell.

So what's a presenter to do? First off, I think that we all need to sit down and have a quick reality check. Why do we give presentations? These are actually pretty poor ways of teaching certain types of new material. Adults learn in all sorts of different ways and listening to spoken words (and looking at PowerPoint slides) doesn't do it for most of your audience (especially the younger ones raised on multimedia).

What this means is that you've got to decide why you are REALLY there. The list is pretty short – convince the audience that your view is correct, get them to agree to take some action, educate them on some new piece of information, or simply to amuse them.

Keeping the "back to basics" concept in mind, we should remember that PowerPoint slides don't deliver the presentation by themselves. Instead, their whole reason for being is to help the presenter. It's when we rely on our slides too much that we start to lose our audience.

So can you use a slide that has a lot (but not too much) information on it? The answer is YES. However, you can't spend too much time on it and your certainly can't read the contents of the slide off to your audience. Remember, the slide is a tool, not the presentation itself.

So what should the ideal PowerPoint presentation look like? In a nutshell, it should look like it was designed to support the words that are being spoken. This will involve a lot of visual imagery ("pretty pictures") and SOME detailed slides if they are needed.

It's how the detailed slides are used that will differ from presentations of old. Show the detailed slide, make your point in an unhurried manner, and then move on. Additional information can be provided on your web site, in handouts, or in pod-casts that your audience can use to learn more AFTER your presentation.

Chapter 9

Make Your Audience Sit Up, Take Notice, And Learn At Your Next Presentation

Make Your Audience Sit Up, Take Notice, And Learn At Your Next Presentation

Some presentations are designed to simply motivate your audience. Some are designed to educate them. It's this second batch that is tricky to do. It's probably not that your presentations are lacking in educational material, but rather it's the way that you are delivering it that really matters. You need to find a way to deliver the information in the way that adults learn…

So here's the answer to this question right off the bat: research shows that adults learn best when information is presented interactively, using role-playing, and peer-to-peer dialog. The lectures that most presenters use are really only good for passing information along to an audience.

The last thing in the world that you want is for your next presentation to remind your audience of a high school or college class. Having you stand at the front of the room and drone on with no chance for interaction is not what today's audiences are looking for.

The secret to making your presentation "stick" with your audience is to realize that the more active your adult audience is during your presentation, the more they will learn because they will be tapping into the knowledge and experience of their peers.

At different times during your presentation your role as the presenter should really be to be a "guide on a side" who facilitates discussions among audience members and offering feedback as needed.

We've all heard about left-brain / right-brain stuff. Our left-brain is set up for the way most presentations are delivered – logical, analytical, and subjective. It's our right-brain, our visual & creative side, that is not being fed during most presentations.

Much of what it takes to make sure that a presentation appeals to how your adult audience learns has to do with how the presentation event is set up. Here are some key suggestions on how you can make your next presentation a powerful adult learning experience:

- **Use Round Tables**: Having your audience sit at round (or half round) tables that seat 8 or 10 people helps your audience to interact easily.

- **Schedule Break Time**: Make sure that your audience has time both before and after your presentation to meet and discuss what they are going to learn and what they have learned.

- **Use Comfortable Seats**: Rarely do we have control over this, but if possible the more comfortable the seats are, the more learning will happen.

- **Lose The Lectern**: This can be done as simply as making sure that you have a wireless microphone so that you are not tied to one spot and can move around and interact with your audience.

- **Handouts & Downloads Are Good**: You audience is hungry for information that they can take back to the office. Giving them something that they can touch and hold is one way to do this.

- **More Brian Food**: This is my favorite. Most food that is served during a presentation can be sugar or carb-heavy. If possible, provide healthful food options.

At the end of the day, you go to a lot of effort to get ready to deliver a presentation. You want your audience to be impacted by your words and you want them to be able to absorb and learn from the information that you are presenting. If you follow these tips, your audience will have a better chance of learning and retaining what you have to say.

Chapter 10

7 Secrets To Getting Your Adult Audience To Learn From Your Presentation

7 Secrets To Getting Your Adult Audience To Learn From Your Presentation

So why should anyone take the time to attend your presentation? Unless you are Paris Hilton (hi Paris!) or former President Clinton, you probably don't have enough star power alone to pull people to your presentation. So what's a presenter to do?

These days with everyone being overworked and so stressed for time, the one question that needs to be answered is "W.I.I.F.M."? That is "What's In It For Me" of course. Another way of saying this is, what are you going to teach me? This brings up the question of just how does a presenter go about teaching an adult audience?

When in doubt, ask an expert. In this case we can have a talk with Dorothy Billington who has done a lot of research into how adults learn. Let's see what her seven secrets to getting adults to learn better are:

1. **Provide A Safe Environment**: In order for students to learn, they need a safe and supportive environment where they are acknowledged and respected.

2. **Be Free To Think**: provide the audience with the ability to experiment and to be creative. This includes having the ability to experience intellectual freedom.

3. **Teacher / Student Interaction**: As a presenter, you need to treat your audience as peers. This means that you need to acknowledge that they are intelligent and experienced adults. You will need to listen to and appreciate their opinions.

4. **Self-Learning**: Your audience must be allowed to take responsibility for their own learning. This means that their learning should be self-directed. Taking the time before your presentation to work with members of the

audience to find out what individual learning needs are will help move this along.

5. **Not Too Fast, Not Too Slow**: As the presenter, you are going to need to come up with the ideal pacing for your audience. This will challenge them at a level that is just beyond their level of their ability. Be careful: if you push the pace too fast, then you'll lose your audience. If your pace is too slow, then you'll bore them.

6. **Make Active Learners**: When your audience is actively involved in the learning process, then they will retain what you say. If they are just sitting there passively, then retention will be less.

7. **Feedback Is Good**: providing a way for your audience to give you feedback on what works for them. Once you start to get this type of input, then you will need to listen to your audience and go back and make changes to your presentation.

Since we've gone to all of the effort of creating a presentation, we need to do our best to make sure that the information sticks with your audience. These seven secrets will get you moving down the right path...

Chapter 11

The Presenter's Dilemma: 5 Ways To Make Your Training Stick

The Presenter's Dilemma: 5 Ways To Make Your Training Stick

Ok, so it's time to talk about an ugly little secret that nobody who does presentations really like to talk about. What's the secret? Most of the time what we tell our audience goes in one ear and out the other. It just doesn't stick.

In fact, if you are presenting training or a new way of doing business to an audience, some studies have shown that only 10% – 40% of what you tell your audience will ever be used by them on the job. Ouch! What are we doing wrong?

Dr. Harry Martin teaches at Cleveland State University in (of course) Cleveland. He is an expert in both management and labor relations. He's got some thoughts on what is going wrong here…

Take heart – it's probably not all about you. When we try to train our audiences, we are really talking about having them change their lives. Change has the unfortunate side effect of creating anxiety in our audience and they will actively seek to avoid change at almost any cost. So is this a losing game?

Good news – the answer is no. However, you've got to start doing some additional work. You need to make sure that a workplace environment that will actively encourage your audience to continue to change is set up and exists long after your presentation is over. In a nutshell, this means that the training can't end when your audience walks out the door. So what's the trick to doing this?

It turns out that there are five simple things that you can either do during your presentation or cause to occur after your presentation is over that will dramatically boost the use of the information that you delivered:

- **Write It Down!**: Everyone should recognize this one from all of those goal setting / time management programs that we're always studying – just getting your audience to write an action plan on how they are going to use what you've covered makes it more likely that they'll do it.

- **This Will Be On The Test**: If you tell your audience that they are going to be tested on the material that you'll be talking about, then they are much more likely to use what you are talking about. The test doesn't have to be a written test, it can be as simple as having them observed and given feedback on their performance. I like it best when the audience is measured before your presentation and then two times afterwords – this always seem to produce the greatest results.

- **Peer Pressure Is Good**: It turns out that having your audience get back together in "peer meetings" is a great way to have them self-motivate to use what you've taught them. What's even more interesting is that this works even better when your audience's management is only lukewarm in their support for your message.

- **Boosting Bosses**: Having managers who are both supportive and actively involved does a lot to increase the odds that your audience will retain and use what you've taught them. This, of course, means that you are going to need to make sure that the bosses are involved in your training.

- **Ask The Expert**: Finally, having the ability to reach out and ask an expert for help in solving a sticky issue or resolving a problem goes a long way in helping your audience use what you've told them. More often than not, you are the expert – make sure that you make arrangements so that you can be contacted after your presentation is over and done with.

Chapter 12

Just How Do Those Politicians Do It?

Just How Do Those Politicians Do It?

Love 'em or hate 'em, politicians are by and large **fantastic communicators**. If you take a look at their technique they may be lacking; however, they sure seem to be very good at getting their point across and wining audiences over. Wouldn't it be great if we could figure out how they do that?

There are a number of speaking techniques that politicians use, but the one that packs the biggest punch is our old friend **the story**. Caren Neile has done some research into just how politicians use stories and she's discovered some things that we can use to make our presentations even better.

Ronald Reagan was known as the great communicator due in a large part to the numerous stories that he would tell. He wasn't just telling stories to fill space in his speeches, rather he was trying to **make points and emphasis parts** of his speech.

For politicians, there are **four main story-lines** that they use over and over:

1. We take care of our own.

2. We must protect ourselves from our enemies.

3. We can't trust the people who are running government and business.

4. Anyone can succeed.

The reason that these four story-lines are used is because they are time tested – politicians know that **they work**, audiences respond to them every time.

For us speakers, we can take advantage of the years of research that politicians have done for us and start to **use more stories**. We can use the four story-lines that have served our leaders so well for so long and create our own stories that flow in these well-worn ruts. By doing this we almost assure ourselves of being successful with our audiences.

Hard work does not
guarantee success;
However, success does
not happen
without hard work.

— Dr. Jim Anderson

Create Speeches That Motivate Your Audiences And Get Your Message Heard!

Dr. Jim Anderson is available to provide training and coaching on the topics that are the most important to people who have to speak in public: how can I create a speech that people want to hear and how can I deliver in a way that will allow me to connect with my audience and get my point across to them?

Dr. Anderson believes that in order to both learn and remember what he says, speakers need to laugh. Each one of his speeches is full of fun and humor so that what he says "sticks" with everyone.

Dr. Anderson's Public Speaking Training Includes:

1. How to plan your next speech: pick your purpose and understand your audience.
2. What's the best way to get PowerPoint and Keynote to work with you, not against you?
3. What do you need to do when you are presenting in order to truly connect with your audience?

Dr. Jim Anderson presents over 100 speeches per year. To invite Dr. Anderson to speak at your event, contact him at: **Phone: 813-418-6970** or **Email:** jim@BlueElephantConsulting.com

Photo Credits:

Cover - By: InteliusInc
http://www.flickr.com/photos/inteliusgal/

Chapter 1 - By: http://www.homespothq.com
http://www.flickr.com/photos/86639298@N02/

Chapter 2 - By: Nick Webb
http://www.flickr.com/photos/nickwebb/

Chapter 3 - By: Gerry Brague
http://www.flickr.com/photos/revger/

Chapter 4 - By: Antonio Furno
http://www.flickr.com/photos/antoniofurno/

Chapter 5 - By: DUP Photos
http://www.flickr.com/photos/dupphotos/

Chapter 6 - By: Daniel Langer
http://www.flickr.com/photos/dlanger/

Chapter 7 - By: Elio Assuncao
http://www.flickr.com/photos/yodspica/

Chapter 8 - By: Paul Hudson
http://www.flickr.com/photos/pahudson/

Chapter 9 - By: Innovation_School
http://www.flickr.com/photos/innovationschool/

Chapter 10 - By: Newman University
http://www.flickr.com/photos/newmanuniversity/

Chapter 11 - By: Bjorn Hermans
http://www.flickr.com/photos/bhermans/

Chapter 12 - By: Penn State

http://www.flickr.com/photos/pennstatelive/

www.ingramcontent.com/pod-product-compliance
Lightning Source LLC
Chambersburg PA
CBHW071820170526
45167CB00003B/1387